PLANETS IN OUR SOLAR SYSTEM

Learn About EARTH!

BY NATALIE HUMPHREY

Enslow PUBLISHING

DISCOVER!

Please visit our website, www.enslow.com. For a free color catalog of all our high-quality books, call toll free 1-800-398-2504 or fax 1-877-980-4454.

Cataloging-in-Publication Data

Names: Humphrey, Natalie.
Title: Learn about Earth! / Natalie Humphrey.
Description: New York : Enslow Publishing, 2024. | Series: Planets in our solar system | Includes index.
Identifiers: ISBN 9781978533493 (pbk.) | ISBN 9781978533509 (library bound) | ISBN 9781978533516 (ebook)
Subjects: LCSH: Earth (Planet)–Juvenile literature.
Classification: LCC QB631.4 H857 2024 | DDC 525–dc23

Portions of this work were originally authored by Daisy Allyn and published as *Earth: The Blue Planet.* All new material in this edition authored by Natalie Humphrey.

Published in 2024 by
Enslow Publishing
2544 Clinton Street
Buffalo, NY 14224

Designer: Andrea Davison-Bartolotta
Editor: Natalie Humphrey

Photo credits: Cover (Earth), p. 1 (Earth) 24K-Production/Shutterstock.com; cover (top), p. 1 (top), series art (backgrounds) Jurik Peter/Shutterstock.com; series art (lens flare) andruxevich/Shutterstock.com; p. 4 Natee Jitthammachai/Shutterstock.com; p. 5 Dima Zel/Shutterstock.com; p. 7 EreborMountain/Shutterstock.com; p. 9 (full moon) Fernando Astasio Avila/Shutterstock.com; p. 9 (new moon) laisva/Shutterstock.com; p. 11 leeborn/Shutterstock.com; p. 12 Ellen Bronstayn/Shutterstock.com; p. 13 NOPPHARAT539/Shutterstock.com; p. 15 Deni_Sugandi/Shutterstock.com; p. 17 DG-Studio/Shutterstock.com; p. 19 Rost9/Shutterstock.com; p. 21 robin2/Shutterstock.com;

Printed in the United States of America

CPSIA compliance information: Batch #CS24ENS: For further information contact Enslow Publishing, at 1-800-398-2504.

CONTENTS

Blue Planet 4
A Year on Earth 6
The Moon 8
Earth's Atmosphere 10
Earth's Crust 12
Always Moving 14
The Mantle 16
The Core 18
Pangaea 20
Words to Know 22
For More Information 23
Index 24

Boldface words appear in Words to Know.

Blue PLANET

There are eight planets in our solar system. Our home planet, Earth, is the third planet from the sun! There's a lot of things that make Earth a very special place. Earth is the only planet that can **support** life as we know it!

Earth is the fifth-largest planet in our solar system.

A Year on EARTH

What is a year? A year is the amount of time it takes for a planet to **orbit** the sun. One year on Earth is around 365 days. While it orbits, Earth spins too. It takes about 24 hours for Earth to spin completely around! This is one day.

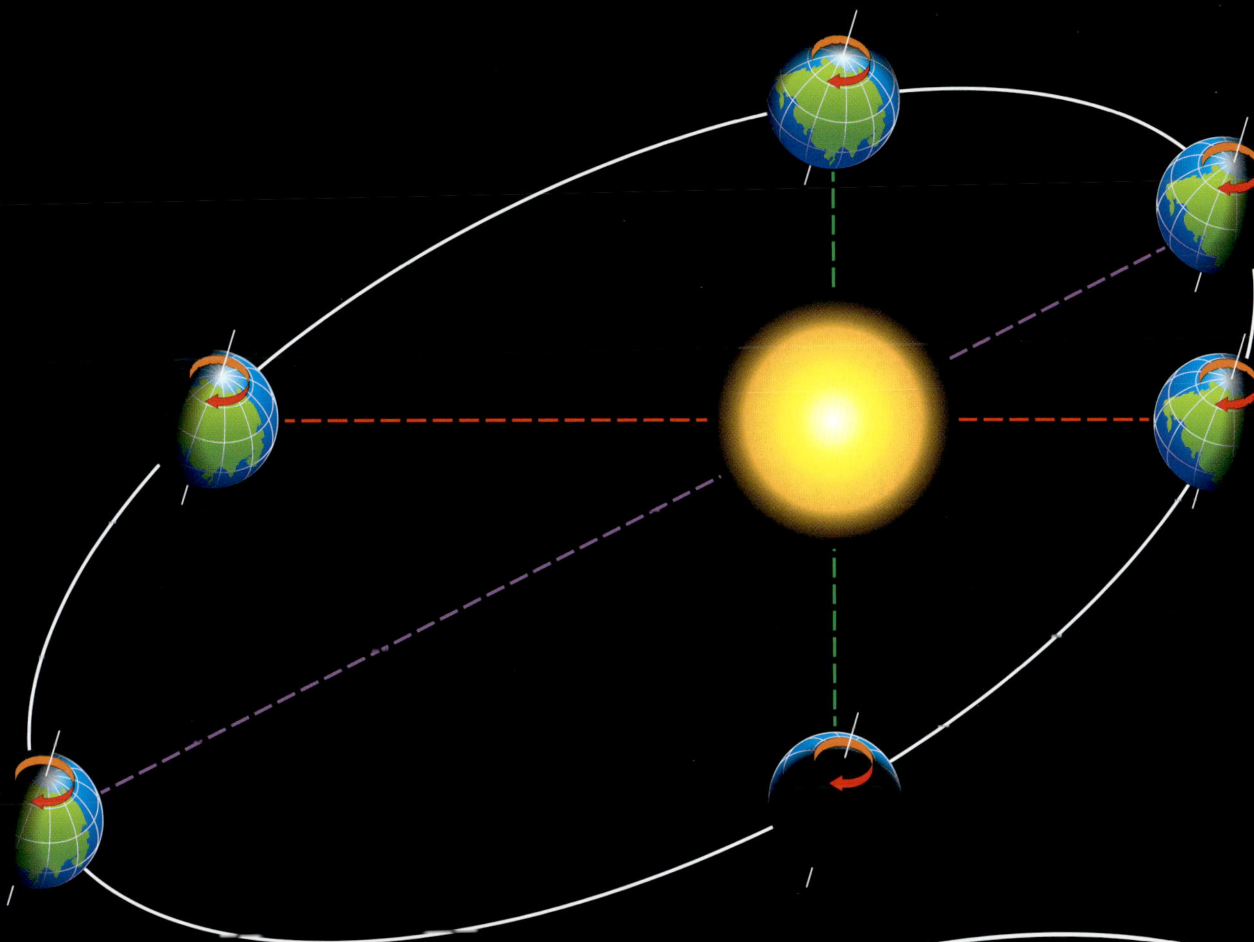

Earth's orbit is elliptical, meaning it is shaped a bit like an oval.

The moon also orbits, but the moon orbits Earth instead of the sun. It takes the moon about 27 days to move all the way around Earth. As the moon orbits, it looks different to us on Earth's **surface**. These differences are called the phases of the moon!

Even though the moon looks different, we always see the same side of the moon from Earth!

Earth's ATMOSPHERE

Earth has a very special **atmosphere**. Earth's atmosphere is made up of mostly the gases oxygen and nitrogen. Because of Earth's atmosphere, plants can live, and animals and people can breathe. There is no other planet we know of that has an atmosphere like Earth's!

Earth's atmosphere is about 78 percent nitrogen and 21 percent oxygen.

Earth's CRUST

Earth is made of different layers. The first layer is called the crust. Earth's crust is made of different kinds of rock. Even though it looks thick to us, the crust is Earth's thinnest layer!

What does the crust look like where you live?

Always MOVING

Even though it's hard to see, Earth's crust is moving! It usually moves too slowly for us to tell, but scientists can tell in a few ways. One is that Earth's **landscape** changes slowly over many years. These changes can cause **earthquakes** and **volcanoes**!

Pieces of Earth's crust move about 0.6 inch (1.5 cm) a year.

The MANTLE

Beneath the crust is the mantle. The mantle is the thickest layer of Earth. It is about 84 percent of its volume, or the amount of space it takes up. Earth's mantle is made of **magma** and is very hot! It can be up to 6,700°F (3,700°C).

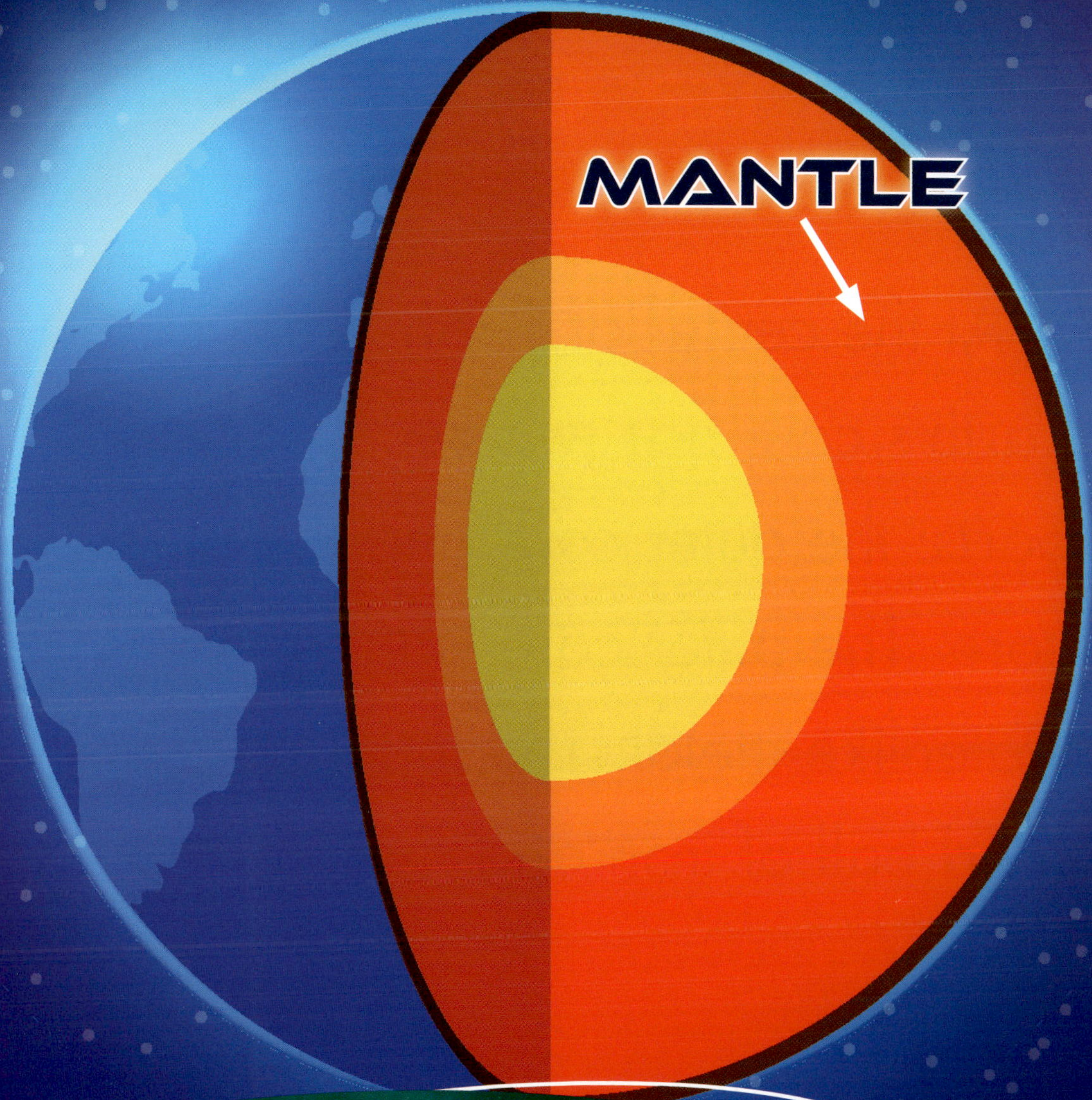

Earth's mantle is around 1,800 miles (2,900 km) thick.

The CORE

At the center of Earth is the core. Earth's core has two sections, or parts: the outer core and the inner core. The outer core is made of water-like metal. The inner core is a solid ball of iron and nickel!

Every year, the core grows about .03 inch (1 mm).

PANGAEA

Around 300 million years ago, scientists believe Earth looked much different than it does today. Instead of being seven **continents** separated by oceans, scientists believe all the continents used to be squished together. This huge group of continents was called Pangaea!

PANGAEA

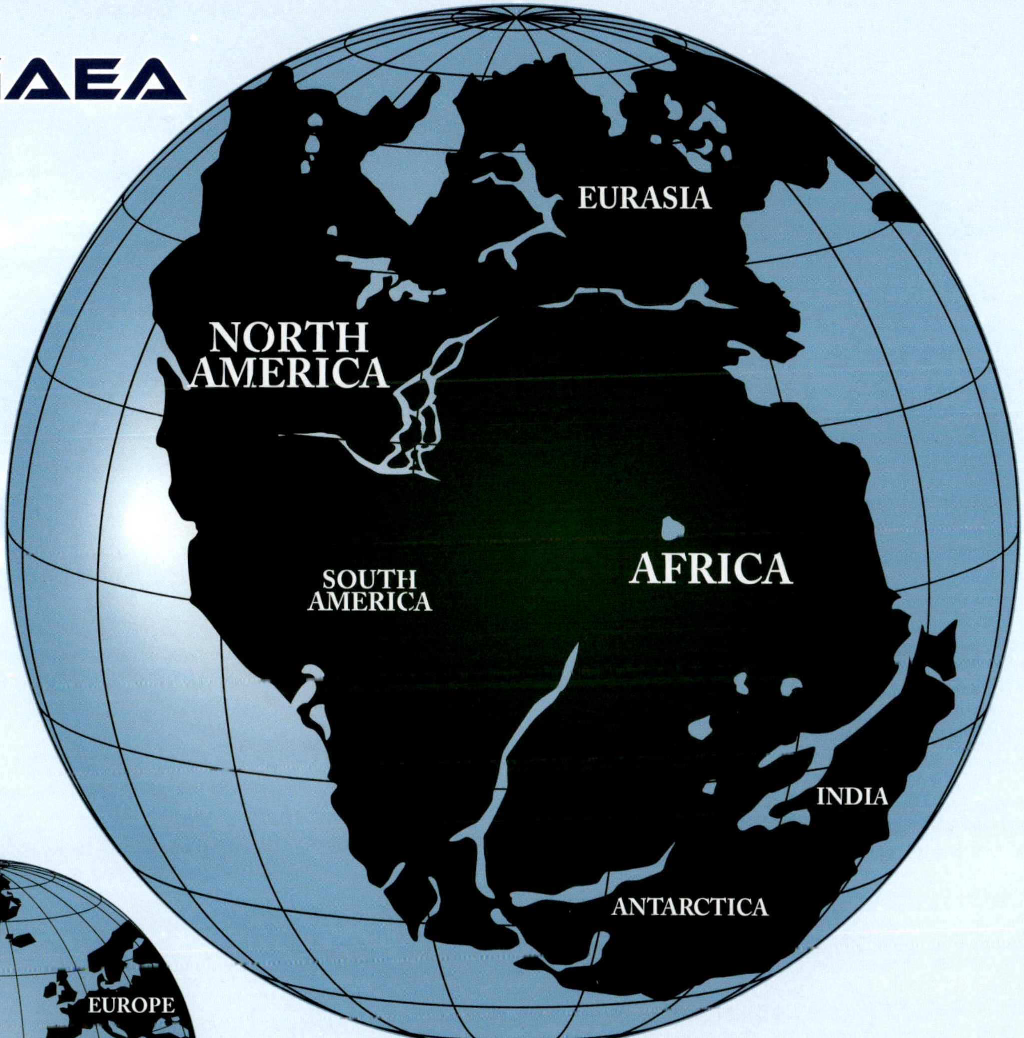

TODAY

The word Panagea comes from the Greek word *pangaia*, meaning "all the Earth!"

WORDS TO KNOW

atmosphere: The mixture of gases that surround a planet.

continent: One of Earth's seven great landmasses.

earthquake: A shaking of the ground caused by the movement of Earth's crust.

landscape: A section of land that all has a certain appearance.

magma: Hot, liquid rock inside Earth.

orbit: To travel in a circle or oval around something.

support: To help.

surface: The top layer of something.

volcano: An opening in a planet's surface through which hot, liquid rock sometimes flows.

FOR MORE INFORMATION

BOOKS

Spencer, Francis. *Earth and Our Solar System*. New York, NY: Crabtree Publishing Company, 2023.

Turner, Myra Faye. *Unsolved Questions About Earth*. North Mankato, MN: Capstone Press, 2023.

WEBSITES

NASA Space Place

spaceplace.nasa.gov/all-about-earth/en/

Check out more pictures, fun facts, and learn more about our home planet from NASA!

National Geographic Kids

kids.nationalgeographic.com/space/article/mission-to-earth

Watch videos and check out more fun facts about planet Earth.

Publisher's note to educators and parents: Our editors have carefully reviewed these websites to ensure that they are suitable for students. Many websites change frequently, however, and we cannot guarantee that a site's future contents will continue to meet our high standards of quality and educational value. Be advised that students should be closely supervised whenever they access the internet.

INDEX

day, 6, 8

iron, 18

layers, 12

life, 4, 10

moon, phases of, 8

nickel, 18

oceans, 12, 20

pangaia, 21

rock, 12

scientists, 14, 16, 20

size, 5

solar system, 4, 5

spin, 6

sun, 4, 6, 8

volume, 16